1976

American Primitive

Teotihuacán culture
Funerary mask covered with mosaic
Museo preistorico Luigi Pigorini, Rome

American Primitive

PEEBLES ART LIBRARY   **Sandy Lesberg, Editor**

First published 1974
by
Peebles Press International
U.S.: 140 Riverside Drive, New York, N.Y. 10024
U.K.: 12 Thayer Street, London, W1M 5LD

ISBN 0-85690-028-1

Illustrations provided by:
Jean Willemin, Paris: pages 8, 10, 12, 16, 18, 20 (upper), 23, 28,
29, 34, 36 (upper), 38, 39, 41, 43.
Zoltan Wegner, London: pages 9, 15, 20 (lower), 21, 24, 25, 26,
30 (right), 37, 40, 42, 47, 48.
Bibliovision Rencontre, Paris: pages 7, 13, 27, 45.
Giraudon, Paris: pages 17, 30 (left), 31, 32, 35, 46.
Jean-Clarence Lambert: pages 19, 22, 44.
Scala, Florence: pages 3, 33.
J.-A. Lavaud, Holmes-Lebel, Paris: pages 11, 14.
Christian Baugey: page 36 (lower).

The illustrations on pages 9, 15, 20 (lower), 21, 23, 24, 25, 26, 37,
47 and 48 are reproduced by kind permission of the British Museum,
London: those on pages 30 (right), 40 and 42 by kind permission
of the Horniman Museum, London.

Distributed by
Walden Books, Resale Division in the
U.S. and Canada.
WHS Distributors in the U.K., Ireland,
Australia, New Zealand and South Africa.

Printed and Bound in Great Britain

Introduction

This book is concerned with Indian America, the America that was nearly ruined for ever by Columbus and his successors, the America that has been concealed rather than revealed by the West, the land of the maize-growers, of the men the colour of maize. From north to south, this country, whose two natural inclinations are the extreme and the excessive, offered the yellow immigrants who came over from Asia via the Bering Strait some of the most astonishing background scenery in the world. And to cover every part of it took thousands of years; thousands of years and an unimaginable series of genetic mutations. Otherwise, how can one consider at the same time the astronomers of Chichén Itzá and the gloomy tribes roaming the heavy humid forests of Brazil, the goldsmiths of the Mixtecs and the salmon-fishers of the Canadian fjords?

In spite of these great differences of material culture, there is a distinct continuity evident among those whom we now call Amerindians, a continuity which runs from north to south, for this seems to have been their ethnic itinerary. First, the Eskimos, who found their destiny in the polar night and the floating world of pack ice: late-comers, the last to set foot on the continent, probably more than eight thousand years after the copper-workers who left their traces in the Great Lakes region. Next, the prehistoric basket-makers of Colorado, the mound-builders of the Mississippi and all those nomads who chose to follow the buffalo through the endless prairies: the Redskins of our childhood dreams. They were the finest hunters ever known, more redoubtable than the wolves themselves and living with a set of moral values which still lurk beneath the façade of modern American society (scouting is the parody and ultimate degradation of the real thing). Down in the hot, damp bay of Vera Cruz lived the Olmecs, a people who still baffle scholars: they provided the groundwork for the civilisation which was to achieve its greatest splendour with the Maya-Nahua culture. (And how better to demonstrate the great burst of creativeness which swept through this chosen part of our planet than to say that, so far, eleven thousand archæological sites have been discovered: eleven thousand centres of civilisation?) Further south still, the narrow neck of the central territories and the scattered islands of the Caribbean ("cleared" of all natives by the first European invasion) lead down to the upsurge of the great central spine. On this side of the equator, the Rockies become the Andes; ten thousand, fifteen thousand feet above the world lies the moon-like landscape of Tiahuanaco, Cuzco, capital of the Tahuantinsuyu, the Empire of the Four Directions. The hellish humidity of Amazonia rolls to its conclusion at the foot of this great mountain barrier: Amazonia, the hothouse jungle in which have grown 19,619 of the 27,767 known species of plants! And the men who live there—who can say how many there are or what they are like? Explorers and ethnographers alike admit defeat. There are the Jivaro, collectors of shrunken heads, and the Caduveo from the Gran Chaco, closely and carefully studied by Claude Levi-Strauss. And the Tupi from Brazil, distant relatives of the Uru from Lake Titicaca, floating to oblivion on balsa islands, and the Quechua, descended from a line of kings but now dying from soroche, the illness of the Andes that only the perpetual and soul-destroying consumption of coca leaves can relieve.

So far, we know very little of the legacy the Amerindians left us, we who belong to a civilisation which strikes mortal blows even in its own death throes. Modern humanists have welded Europe to Asia to form a spiritual ambience embracing every philosophy. But supposing this enormous synthesis were incomplete—what then? Leaving Africa on one side (in spite of the revelation it has provided in the world of art), supposing the Amerindians had some message of universal import to offer us? For those who have found this suggestion immediately acceptable and who have tried to support it with facts, there is no doubt about it. The higher civilisations of America are among the greatest ever evolved on earth. On the spiritual level, the worship of Quetzalcoatl, the finest expression of ancient Mexico, can be compared with any complex of beliefs developed in Eurasia. In the field of collective organisation, the Incas put into practice one of the least bad socialist systems so far evolved. As for the development of men as individuals, far from being made into vague members of one great indistinct herd (which was exactly what the Europeans wanted to turn the Indians into), it is known now that the Amerindians were exceptionally successful in keeping themselves as individuals rather than as parts of a collective entity. This is surely what Antonin Arnaud meant when he said that the Tarahumaras of the Mexican Sierra Madre "spread their knowledge throughout the whole organism". By using a variety of initiation rites and painful ordeals as well as by using drugs which stimulated both mind and body to unexpected ends, the Indians brought their being into harmony with the world in a far more fundamental way than we have ever known. Was this not a direct answer to pain and suffering such as Job and Buddha could not make? Arnaud went on to say: "Like all pure races, it was in their very vitals and their basic senses that the Mexicans managed to carry the culture which was to become a superb and delicate refinement of sensitivity."

The aptitudes of Maya and Inca for the sciences, the Amerindian gift for literary expression—even though they used no true system of writing (the Eskimos are such gifted poets that Eluard claimed they influenced him—the Algonquins were inexhaustible story-tellers and the Nahuas left a superb and wholly inexhaustible body of literature), the passion for building which is demonstrated so magnificently by Palenque, Macchu Picchu, Chavín, Teotihuacán, Tikal and La Venta: there was nothing they could not conceive and carry through. Nowhere is this more evident than in the plastic arts, for here the skilful hands of Amerindian artists moulded, plaited, wove, carved and engraved. In the field of drawing and painting alone, from the crude petroglyphs of the Arizona Zuñi to the powerful frescoes of Bonampak, from Chimú and Nazca pottery to body painting or the decorated tepees of Apache warriors, the variety of both style and content is bewildering. Certain features are constant throughout and they are those common to all artistic achievement at the same cultural level. There is, for instance, a firm distinction between naturalism and geometrism, the latter being peculiarly the women's province and the former the men's—at least in groups where the artist's function was not held to be a specialised one. But a purely formal analysis, here more than anywhere else, would be unacceptable: the elements on which their aesthetic is based are secondary, almost accessory to the main cause. The true artistic categories are those of good and evil, what is good and what is bad. Amerindian painting is, in the fullest meaning of the word, a code which must be deciphered. Forms and colours have a very precise meaning which cannot be ignored. Alas, it is to ignorance that we are most often condemned, to the ignorance of onlookers who have come too far too late!

Our only solution would seem to be to try to recapture that dream state which, deep inside each one of us, harbours primitive man, discovered by the archæologists of the unconscious who have revealed to us the long-lost, long-forgotten civilisations of the mind.

Jean-Clarence Lambert

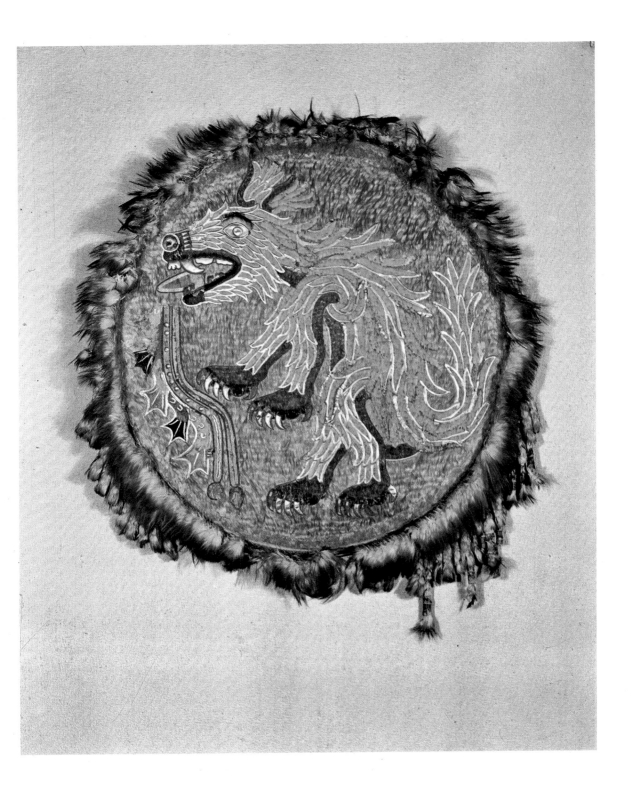

Aztec civilisation, post-classic
15th century
Feather shield, 27 in. diameter
Museum für Völkerkunde, Vienna

Paracas Necropolis
Detail from embroidered burial cloth
Private collection, USA

Oyana, Guiana
Cloth decorated with feathers
British Museum, London

Mochica
Private collection,
Paris

Kuskokwim, end 19th century
Eskimo mask, painted wood and feathers
Height 28 in.
Former André Breton Collection, Paris

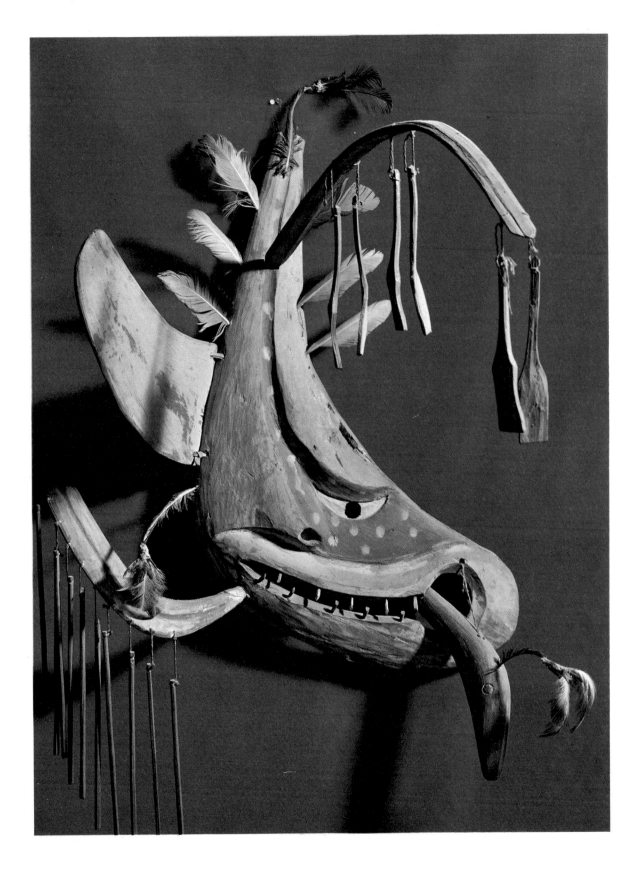

Chilcat, British Columbia
Ceremonial cape with totemic decoration
Charles Ratton Collection, Paris

Mixteca-Puebla culture
Gold vase representing the god Xipe-Totec
Oaxaca Museum

Eskimo mask, painted wood and feathers
Private collection, Paris

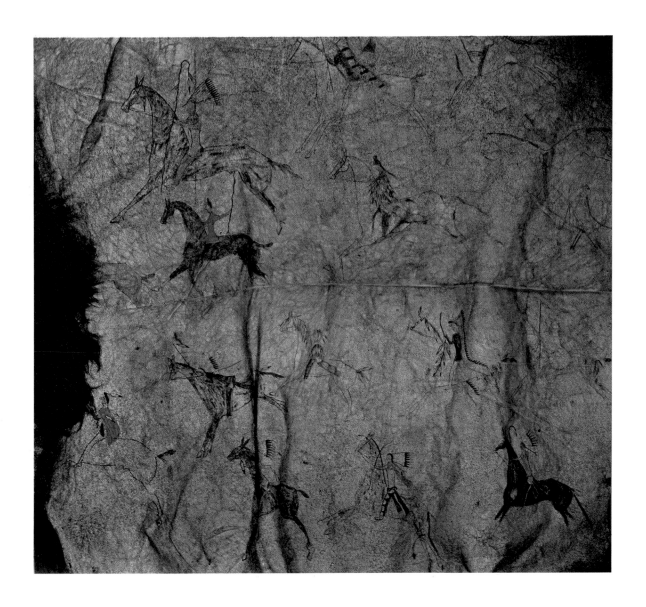

Plains Indians
Buffalo hide with figure decoration
About 1880, 103 in. long
British Museum, London

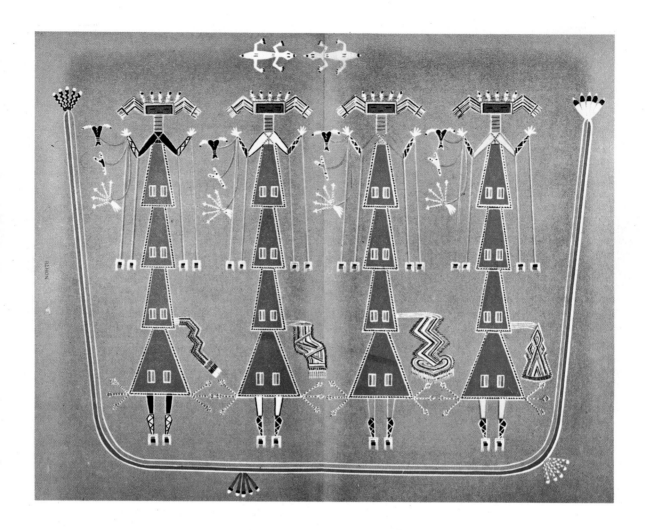

Navajo
Sand painting
Private collection, Paris

Ancient Maya civilisation (A.D. 600-950)
Large cylindrical vase, with relief-moulded head
of the Sun
Ochre terracotta with traces of fresco
painting 20 × 13 in.
Museum of Ethnography, Vienna

Central America, Costa Rica
Polychrome tripod vase shaped
like an animal
Height 16 in.
Charles Ratton Collection, Paris

Orchestral piece: *Three musicians
playing the Sonaja*
Mural painting, detail
Bonampak, first room, east wall

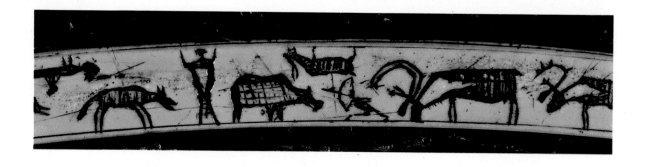

Eskimo art
Engraved ivory
Charles Ratton Collection, Paris

Haida, British Columbia
Chest with symbolic decoration
British Museum, London

Eskimo mask, painted wood and feathers
British Museum, London

Two people in the procession engaged in conversation
Mural painting, detail
Bonampak, first room, north wall

British Columbia
Models of Haida totems
Painted wood, height 17 in. and 10 in.
Private collection, Paris

British Columbia
Articulated mask with four opening flaps
Georges Duthuit Collection, Paris

Vancouver Island, British Columbia, Kwakiutl
Thunderbird, totem
British Museum, London

Paracas Necropolis
Border of burial cloth
British Museum, London

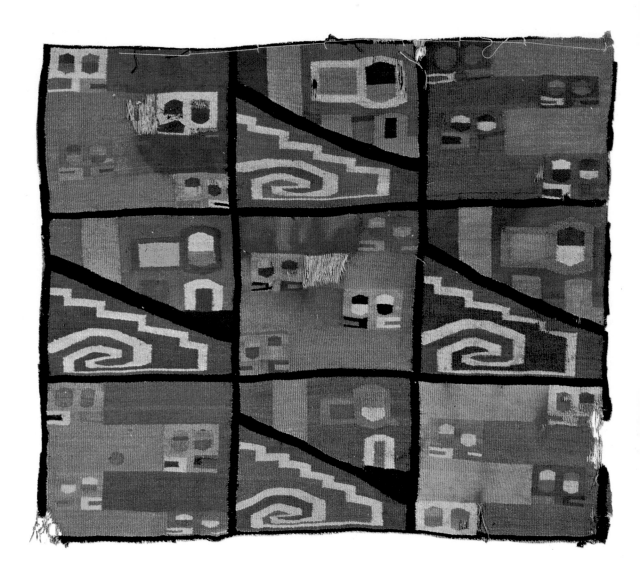

Tiahuanaco
Burial cloth
British Museum, London

Mochica
Stirrup-spout vase
Musée de l'Homme, Paris

Aztec civilisation
Poncho with feather decoration
Georges Duthuit Collection, Paris

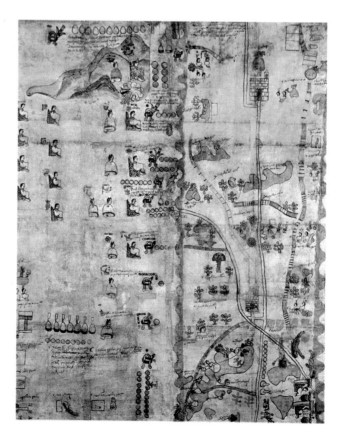

Late Aztec
Trial scene
Charles Ratton Collection, Paris

Mixtec
Codex Becker I, folio 5 (detail)
Museum of Ethnography, Vienna

Ancient Maya civilisation (A.D. 600-950)
Ochre terracotta with traces of painting 11 × 4 in.
National Museum of Anthropology, Mexico City

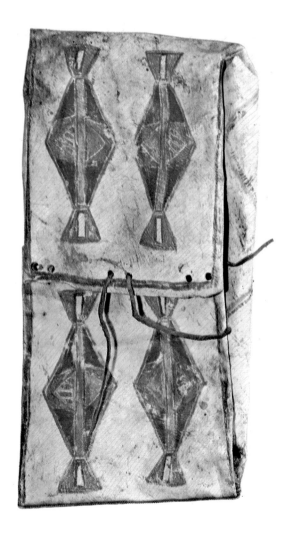

Yakima, Plains Indians
Travelling bag, folded 27 × 11 in.
Horniman Museum, London

Ancient Maya civilisation (A.D. 600-950)
Terracotta 6 × 3 in.
Private collection, Mexico City

Aztec civilisation (A.D. 1324-1521)
Shield made as a mosaic of feathers showing
the head of a god
National Museum of Anthropology, Mexico

Aztec or Mixtec civilisation
Wooden mask covered with turquoise
and coloured shell mosaic
Height 7 in.
Museo preistorico, Rome

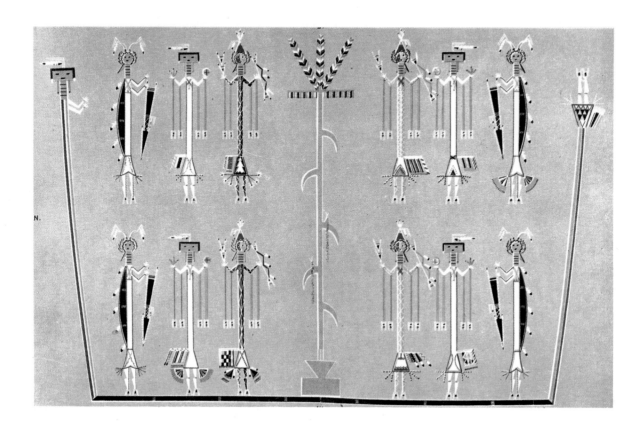

N.

Navajo
Sand painting
Private collection, Paris

Toltec culture (A.D. 856-1168)
Atlantean figure with raised arms
Painted basalt 32 × 16 in.
National Museum of Anthropology, Mexico City

Paracas Necropolis
Detail from embroidered burial cloth
Private collection, USA

Pachacamac
Painted textile
Museo Puno, Lima (Peru)

Central America, Costa Rica
Polychrome receptacle in the shape of a bird
British Museum, London

Mochica
Charles Ratton Collection,
Paris

Hopi
Katchina doll
Painted cottonwood
Height 8 in. (without feathers)
Horniman Museum, London

Haida, British Columbia
Rattle in the shape of a seal's head
Horniman Museum, London

Vancouver, British Columbia
Dish in the shape of a boat, length 12 in.
Horniman Museum, London

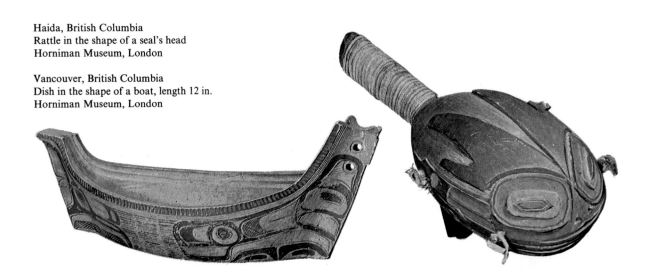

Marajó, Amazonia
Female figure
Terracotta, height 9 in.
Private collection, Paris

Amazonia
Funerary vessels from the "Hernmarck" Mound,
Mojos, Bolivia
Private collection, Paris

Vancouver Island, British Columbia, Kwakiutl
Top: hat made from woven cedar bark
24 in. diameter
Bottom: cloak made from woven cedar bark
Horniman Museum, London

Hopi Katchina gods
Keme, Siwap, Hotcani, Tawa
drawn by an Indian about 1885
Private collection, Paris

KEME

HOTCANI

SIWAP

TAWA

*The God of Rain distributing his gifts in the form
of precious objects in jade* (detail)
Mural painting
Teotihuacán, Tetitla, Portico of the Patio

Maya civilisation, 8th century
Fresco, detail
Temple of Paintings, Bonampak
Bonampak (Chiapas State, Mexico)

Maya-Toltec civilisation
Chichén Itzá
Mosaic-work shield
National Museum of Anthropology, Mexico City

Central America, Cuñas
Blouse decorated with stylised lizard
British Museum, London

Mochica
Stirrup-spout vase
British Museum, London

Glossary of American Primitive Art

Apache

An Athapaskan tribe, warlike, rapacious and nomadic. Early in the first centuries A.D. they migrated from the far north of America and settled in the south, conquering the more peaceful Pueblos. The modern Navajos were originally a tribe of Apache from Nabajù who decided to settle down alongside their Pueblo neighbours. From the Mexican frontier to the Mississippi plains, these wild, wandering tribes maintained a continuous relationship between the culture of the Plains Indians and that of the South-West. Like the Pueblos, they were skilled basketmakers and learnt the art of painting on deerskin from the Plains Indians. They resisted the Spaniards at Cochise, and when they broke into open revolt at Santa Fé in 1693 the struggle ended with the release of countless horses: these turned wild and provided the Plains Indians with their most useful means of resistance. Apache and Navajo now live in reserves in Oklahoma, Arizona and New Mexico.

Arawak

Linguistic group from South America. The Arawak-speaking Indians seem to be the descendants of an old civilisation which stretched from the northern Andes and Amazonia to the West Indies. Paul Rivet claims that they invented the copper-gold alloy known as *tumbaga* which the goldsmiths of Colombia and Central America used so skilfully.

Articulated masks

Masks with movable sections were produced in all the tribes of the North-West coast of North America. It was however the Kwakiutl who made the most splendid and original versions of this art form. They used the masks for initiation ceremonies into their secret societies. They were made by initiates working in great secrecy and under close surveillance and were a particularly spectacular accessory in the marvellously theatrical scenes where skilled performers manipulated flaps, bellows and invisible strings. Articulated masks fall into two categories. In the first, only the eyes and lower jaw are movable. The second type open into two, three or four sections to expose a second face below the first. All the mobile sections are controlled by strings.

Athapaskans

Linguistic group from North America, now represented by the Alaska Athapaskans and the Apache and Navajo tribes in the south-western part of the United States.

Bering, Vitus (1680-1741)

Danish sailor. In 1728, Bering explored the Bering Sea, bounded on the west by the Kamchatka peninsula, the Koriak mountains, the coast of the Anadyr Gulf and the Chukchi peninsula, and on the south by the Aleutian Islands. It was then that he discovered the strait between Asia and America which gives access to the Arctic Ocean and which now bears his name. The Bering Strait was the seat of an extremely old civilisation which was brought to light in the 1950s. At Okvik and Ipiutak, a series of masks were found, covered in a mosaic of ivory plates and leaves of deer antler. The influences of Chinese bronze age art and Asian shamanism met and gradually fused over a long period, affecting every part of the south Pacific coastline from the Amur basin in the west to Vancouver in the east, ending with a perfect synthesis in Alaska.

Bison

Before the arrival of the English and the French, the great plains which stretch from the Canadian frontier to Texas were the favourite pastures of immense herds of bison whose only enemies were a few tribes of Apaches who hunted them on foot. The capture and taming of horses which had escaped from Spanish ranches gave the Plains Indians the opportunity of abandoning farming for the far more rewarding buffalo hunt; they smoked the surplus meat and this provided plenty of food until the next herds came along. Ceremonies linked to the needs of agriculture gave way to hunting rituals and the buffalo dance was held in great honour in the prairies. Hunting provided the basic materials for their religious ceremonies and gave painters large-sized skins which were used to make tents, ceremonial capes and a variety of objects like shields. The oldest painted buffalo skin known tells the story of the attack made by the Sioux and the Aribara on the Mandan in 1797. During the American Civil War (1860-1865), the systematic machine-gun slaughter of thousands of prairie bison by the commissaries of both North and South caused widespread famine among the Indian tribes.

Body painting

The origin of body painting seems to relate to the darker impulses, but the ritual or habitual use of such paintings has made them into a sort of art form which can afford to ignore its distant past. Few peoples have devoted as much time to their body decoration as the Indians. The Plains Indians in North America always fought with their faces painted red (hence the name Redskin); they performed their sun rituals totally naked apart from a covering of simple yet mysterious painted patterns. In Pre-Columbian Mexico, every ceremony had a special body painting for everyone taking part. This was probably just the same in Peru, where mummies were often painted. Among the Indians of South America who were the most famous for their body paint, one should mention the Chama, the Indians from the Tumuc Humac mountains in Guiana and the Kaduveo from the south of Brazil. For the latter, this was a totally female art: "They lived completely naked," wrote Claude Levi-Strauss, "and spent entire days covering each other's body and face with a network of painted arabesques of an unforgettable delicacy and elegance."

Bonampak

A strange combination of circumstances led to the discovery in 1946 of the almost intact and undamaged frescoes at Bonampak (the word means "painted walls" in modern Maya). Buried in the heart of the tropical forest, this old city from the days of the Maya empire was never discovered by either Mexican or Spanish invaders— nor, indeed, by the 18th- and 19th-century archæologists who excavated the Maya cities. The Bonampak frescoes have been protected by a thick layer of calcite which still makes them far from easy to interpret. They cover the walls and ceilings of three rooms of a small building and they give a much fiercer picture of the Mayas than archæologists had previously known.

Preparations for war, war council, hand-to-hand fighting, processions of prisoners, torture and sacrifice of the conquered, everything suggests that the murals illustrate some famous battle, unless one accepts Eric Thompson's idea that they show a ceremony of sacrifice in honour of the earth demons. These are the most outstanding frescoes to survive from Indian America, but they do not provide any clue to the role the city of Bonampak must have played in the Maya empire right up to the 9th century A.D. Jade and pottery of Mexican origin have been discovered at the site.

" Bourrage "

The practice of filling space with carefully detailed drawings. The term was first used in connection with psychopathological art, and it denoted a desire to capture space by cramming it full of meticulous detail without any regard for the basic laws of artistic composition.

Caribs

We do not know exactly when the Caribs invaded the Antilles, formerly occupied by the Arawaks. They were totally supreme only in the Lesser Antilles. Their language was also spoken on the Guiana coast and is still in use among a few scattered groups in America and in the southern part of the continent.

Cerro de las Mesas

One of the main sites of the La Venta culture, very near Tres Zapotes. The excavations which started in 1938 brought to light a number of steles, some of which have a jaguar-mask carved at the base. Others are carved with hieroglyphics not unlike Zapotec signs. Many jade and diorite objects have been found, together with pottery jars containing the decapitated heads of young men. At Cerro de las Mesas, the last phase of pottery development was influenced by the Highland cultures: it is related to ceramics from Cholula and the Mixtec culture.

Chanchan

The ancient capital of the Chimú Empire near Trujillo in the Moché valley in Northern Peru. In the 14th and 15th centuries, this city, now in ruins, was the home of princes and the religious and secular aristocracy of the empire. From the 16th century onwards the city has been pillaged, but even today gold and silver ornaments are still found in the ruined palaces and temples and tombs. Chanchan was famous for its wealth, and its craftsmen produced great gold pectorals, hammered silver vessels, bowls, vases, sacrificial knives and gold and silver, often encrusted with turquoise and mother-of-pearl to give figurative motifs.

Chavín

The Chavín horizon is the one which contains the Peruvian remains contemporary with those of Chavín de Huantar; this city, in the mountainous regions lying to the east of Callejón de Huayalas, is built around a central area and is composed of rectangular buildings whose walls include stones sculptured in the shape of jaguar heads. A great many engraved stones have been dug out near these buildings. They all have the same ribbon-strip decoration of mythical beings characterised by cat fangs. The elegance of style and technique in Chavín art has led some archæologists to reject the idea that it is the prototype for Cerro Sechín, suggesting instead that it might indeed be the latter which offered the initial development.

Cherokee

Powerful tribe from the east of the United States. They settled in the former territory of the Mound-Builders round about the year A.D. 1000. By the end of the 18th century, they were the members of the Five Civilised Tribes who had made the greatest efforts to resist the colonists by adapting themselves to their way of fighting. In 1827, the Cherokee alphabet was invented by Sequoyah and rapidly spread through the Indian tribes, inaugurating a writing-based culture which disappeared soon afterwards with the great tribes.

Chibcha

Ethnic group probably originating in the highlands in the Bogotá area of Colombia. Many tribes of Chibcha were encountered by the first travellers in Central America, even as far to the north as Lake Nicaragua. The tribes who stayed on the Bogotá plateau are more generally known as Muisca. They formed small independent states where local princes patronised the work of goldsmiths. Their homes were clad in sheets of gold and gave rise to the legend of El Dorado.

Chichén Itzá

Maya site in northern Yucatán; cultural centre of prime importance, characteristic of the Maya "renaissance" (the so-called New Empire) and of Toltec supremacy in Maya territory. A few of the twenty-five or so temples and buildings gathered around the great pyramid of Chichén Itzá (the Spaniards' Castillo) should be mentioned, notably the Snail House (the Cara-

col), which was a Maya observatory, the Well of Sacrifice, the ball-court, the Temple of Warriors (or Jaguars), the Tzompantli (or place of skulls), the Temple of a Thousand Columns, the Mercado. The frescoes in the Temple of the Warriors, now much faded, have a certain calm simplicity, but the bas-reliefs in the ball-court are typical of art from the Mexican highlands, and have much of the brutal impetuosity of the Mixtecs.

Chilkat

Sub-group of the Tlingit family from the North-West coast of North America. The Chilkat, who lived around the fjords in the Juneau region, are known for their woven blankets which gave the art of British Columbia its most systematic aspect. Woven by the women, these textiles derive from southern prototypes created by the Tsimshian.

Cloaks, Ceremonial

Not a single leather cape worn by Mexican dignitaries has survived, but bas-reliefs, frescoes and codices give ample evidence of their superb painted decoration. They were the province of very specialised artists who paid the greatest attention to the correctness of the symbolism, especially if the cloak was to be worn as part of a religious ceremony relating to the incarnation of a god. Among the Plains Indians, chiefs and warriors painted their own buffalo-hide capes with scenes of their own exploits. As recently as the 18th century, the sachems of the Natchez tribe wore capes completely covered in feathers for special days. On similar occasions, the North-West Coast Indians wore emblazoned garments whose designs were achieved by weaving or else were painted on to leather.

Codex

Collections of ancient Mexican pictures. The scenes shown by these paintings are accompanied by hieroglyphic signs and symbols. They show either religious ceremonies, or astronomical events with divinatory significance, or the genealogy of the rulers. The rarity and obscurity of the Mexican and Maya codices is due to the efforts of the Bishop of Landa, who had them publicly burned. The few which escaped destruction are painted, some on deerskin, others on cotton material or sisal paper. These basic materials were prepared by being treated with lime. Almost all are accordion-pleated and painted on both sides. The best-known pre-Conquest codices are the Codex Borbonicus, a Nahuatl calendar now in the Palais-Bourbon (A.D 1450-1520); the Codex Borgia, a Nahuatl astronomical calendar; the Dresden Codex from the Maya "New Empire" (A.D 1000-1300); the Nuttall Codex, a Mixtec historical narrative now in the British Museum; the Codex Vaticanus B, an astronomical and mythological calendar from Cholula; and the Mixtec Codex from Vienna, which is a mythological and historical memorandum. The paintings of these codices provided Mexican artists with their greatest opportunity for powerful and brilliant technical skill.

Cupisnique

Peruvian site in the Chicama valley near Trujillo. Pottery decorated by careful incisions has been found there and this seems to relate to the Chavín period. It was at Cupisnique that stirrup-spout pots were found for the first time. These were to become the most common form of ceramic in the Mochica culture.

Dong-Son

Archæological site in North Vietnam characteristic of the bronze age civilisation which appeared in South-East Asia in about 750 B.C. Dong-Son decoration, an endless juxtaposition of low-relief S-motifs, developed from a very old civilisation from Central Asia. The influences from this old culture account for the development of the art of bronzework in China from the Shang dynasty to the Chou dynasty, when the curves and S-motifs were produced in a higher relief than that used at Dong-Son. The historical importance of Dong-Son decoration has been closely studied by Douglas Fraser, who has shown how it appears in a great many stylistic traditions from Oceania and America.

Double

The "astral body" of Western esoterism. In societies where shamanism is prevalent, the conscious personality and the physical body are not enough to define any particular individual. The life force, interior coherence, powers of expression, magical forces—these are the characteristics of the "double" which lives at the heart of each individual person. Similarly, animals who dispense or who hold magic power also have a double; Eskimos from Kuskokwim depict the double as a human being.

Gateway of the Sun

The Gateway of the Sun is the only part of the great city of Tiahuanaco to escape the depredations of builders anxious to use its stones as building material for La Paz, the nearby capital city of Bolivia. A monolithic carving ten feet high and about fourteen feet wide, it dominates the huge stretch of ruined buildings on the

Tiahuanaco plateau. Its central motif, a divinity in a surrounding nimbus of sun's rays holding in each hand a sceptre surmounted by a condor's head, travelled far and wide as the Tiahuanaco style spread over South America. It is found in the motifs decorating pottery from the coastal Tiahuanaco culture, and here it shows an icy hardness which robs it of depth and emotive power, though it adds somewhat to its intensity. Around this motif, the Gateway of the Sun displays three superimposed friezes which repeat the theme of the winged demon.

Gorgerin

Shell-disc engraved or cut out, four to eight inches in diameter and pierced in two places so that it can be worn hanging over the chest. They are typical products of the Mound-Builder culture and have a variety of decorative motifs: spirals, stylised animals, scenes of fighting and dancing. Some still bear traces of colour. The most interesting gorgerins come from mounds in the Mississippi valley. Both style and subject-matter recall the engraved and perforated mother-of-pearl plaques from the Huaxtec culture.

Guetars

A Chibcha-speaking people who lived in Costa Rica and who are thought to have produced the stone sculptures known as *metates*. These are stone tables used for the ritual grinding of maize. They are in the shape of jaguars, the body of the animal forming the flat table surface. The Guetars also produced highly conventionalized stone figures about 15 inches high. Some scholars think that the Guetars lived in the Antilles before the Arawak.

Guiana

On the vast Guiana plateau which stretches from the Orinoco to the Amazon live numerous tribes speaking different languages, springing from different cultures and living in totally different ways. Sedentary settlers and nomads, Caribs, Arawak, Palicour, all have two things in common: a remarkably uniform concept of shamanism and an equal skill in the art of featherwork. The most beautiful birds in the world impart a richness only equalled in Oceania to their ornaments, headdresses, necklets and cloaks. In the 18th century, the arrival of African negroes gave rise to an Afro-Indian art which used incised motifs closely related to Ashanti art from Ghana.

Haida

Indians from the North-West Coast of North America. They live in the archipelago of the Queen Charlotte Islands; they are reckoned the most warlike of all the northern tribes. Their art achieves sublime grandeur in their totem poles but is remarkably delicate in the carving of smaller objects. However, their finest period was short-lived, and during the 19th century the Haida produced a more naturalistic sculpture of less significance.

Hohokam

Traces of the Hohokam culture have been found along the Gila and Salt rivers in Arizona. Like the Cochise culture which preceded it in the same area, it related to desert farmers who were also skilled potters. Their artistic production is divided by archæologists into four periods which lasted up to A.D. 1400, when the culture gradually died away. The anthropomorphic figurines of the first period were followed by cream-coloured pottery with red decoration. The third period was the finest. Under the name of Sacaton, it revealed breadth of design and variety of form.

Incas

Peruvian tribes from the highlands. Starting in about A.D. 1200, they were ruled by an absolute monarch living at Cuzco. In the 16th century when the Spaniards arrived in Peru, the Inca Empire had become much more strictly organised: it was divided up in strict geometric divisions and ruled over by state-appointed civil servants. The empire included all the territories which went from Colombia to Chile and the eastern Cordillera of the coast. All the provinces ruled from Cuzco had been forced to abandon their own customs in order to integrate themselves with the rigid hierarchy of the Incas. The Incas produced the polychrome Cuzco pottery as well as a variety of vases, the most interesting of which was the *aryballos*. The main decorative theme was the fernleaf.

Iroquois

In a general sense, the Iroquois are Indians who speak the Iroquois tongue. They are the Indians who lived on the coast of the Gulf of Mexico as well as in lodges on the shores of the St Lawrence and in the region to the east of the Great Lakes. They were a warlike people whose ascendancy put an end to the strife between the Iroquois-speaking peoples and brought about the establishment (in 1570) of the Iroquois League, also called the League of the Five Nations or the League of the Great Peace. In the precepts laid down when this league was formed, the Iroquois showed that their views were truly of the highest moral order. In alliance with the English, the league helped to beat the French in the 18th century. Then they joined Washington to participate in the War of Independence. Apart from creating wampum belts, the Iroquois also made masks: their artists belonged to the Society of False Faces and the masks were significant only if carved from the living tree.

Jaguar

Principal deity of the American pantheon, worshipped from Mexico to the southern Andes. The jaguar cult was still practised in the south of Mexico when the Spaniards invaded. The animal appears constantly in La Venta art and is just as omnipresent with the Zapotecs and the Mayas. In Costa Rica and Colombia, it frequently appears in ceramic decoration as well as on carved stone. In Peru, it is a repeated figurative motif in Chavín art. It seems likely that its importance relates to a distant totemic affiliation.

Katchina

Native name for the legendary beings worshipped by the Pueblo Indians. The Katchina live in the other world for half the year. For the other half, they move invisibly among men. The act of wearing a mask during ceremonies in their honour can call forth their invisible presence. The dancers' costumes, the product of a long tradition, are worn by the dolls carved by the Hopi and the Zuñi from softwood; these dolls are commonly called katchinas: by giving them all their usual attributes, they familiarise the children with the legendary beings and allow them to recognise them easily.

Luna

Luna pottery comes from Ometepe Island in Lake Nicaragua. Its style reappears in pottery from scattered sites in Costa Rica and Nicaragua. Although Mexican influence was always strong in the north of these two countries, Luna pottery bears no trace of the symbolism characteristic of Mexico.

Marajó

The island of Marajó, separated from the mainland by the mouth of the Amazon, was deserted when the Portuguese arrived there in the 16th century. Later, a variety of large pieces of pottery were found, but nothing is known of their makers and the way they lived. Archæology has shown that the most recent layers contain pottery whose ornamentation is increasingly rudimentary. Ceramics from the best period have a characteristic network decoration which suggests a distinct Andean influence.

Mitla

Necropolis of the Zapotec civilisation and centre of Mixtec culture. The temple at Mitla owes its outstanding importance to the severity of its ornamentation in which we find an interplay of curves and S-motifs, transformed geometrically into key patterns and step patterns. The Spaniards found many buildings still standing when they came to Mexico, but of all the ones then used by the Mixtec princes, very few still exist. At Mitla we have a series of frescoes painted in red on a white ground very much in the style of the Codex Borgia. They may well be the work of Mixtec artists and are probably anterior to the development of the Aztec civilisation.

Mochica

The Mochica civilisation developed during the classic period of Peruvian culture in the valleys of Moche, Virú and Chicama; the Mochicas owe their reputation to the vast number of realistic ceramics they left in their tombs. Many vessels have survived in perfect condition, unlike the frescoes found in the burial chambers of the pyramids. Those from Moche and Pañamarca show battles between demons.

Monte Alban

Zapotec sanctuary composed of pyramids, observatories and temples standing high above the Oaxaca valley. From the 3rd to the 10th centuries, the influence of Monte Alban spread all over central Mexico. Here, the priests probably used the 260-day year long before the Mayas knew it. The ceramics from Monte Alban have enabled us form a chronological sequence. Its origins show a marked Olmec influence, but in its last days the Mixtecs were supreme. From the Mixtec period come most of the treasures found at Monte Alban, in particular those from tomb no. 7 which have been compared for richness and quantity with those found in the tomb of Tutankhamen. The frescoes from tombs nos. 104, 105 and 125 date from the early days of Mixtec infiltration. They have all the nobility and power of the finest Zapotec ceramics and constantly depict the mythological beings of the Mixtec codices without, however, indulging in their profusion of ornament.

Mound builders

The culture derived from the builders of mounds, embarkments and tumuli spread during the first thousand years A.D. from the Gulf of Mexico to the Great

Lakes. Further classification was brought by 19th-century archæologists, who divided their structures up into effigy mounds, burial mounds, pyramid tumuli and the outer walls of great halls. Many remains provide valuable information about this important culture, and the most informative of all come from Mexico. The Cahokia pyramid in Illinois is now only 100 feet high. The rarity of objects found from this distant period of time adds to their charm, and none is more attractive than the famous Adena pipe, the mother-of-pearl gorgerins from Ohio and the engraved drawings on native copper. In the architectural field, the serpent mound, the bear and the lizard mound are related to a totally different scale in an identical universal concept.

Ninstints

The Ninstints, now extinct, were a branch of the Haida nation which lived on Antony Island in the extreme south part of the archipelago of the Queen Charlotte Islands. A warrior tribe noted for its fierce individuality, they excelled in sculpture. Their totem poles are characterised by a breadth of line and a moving sensitivity.

Nootka

The Nootka lived along the fjords in the western part of Vancouver Island. They were famous for their boldness as whale-hunters. Their expeditions were preceded by a long ceremony which took place in the Whale House, which was painted specially both inside and outside. In the sculpture of totem poles and masks, the Nootka resembled the Eskimos; they were in addition the only Indians in British Columbia to use whalebone for making their masks. Their most characteristic mask represents a wolf-head, and these were worn as part

of a ceremony describing the ritual capture of children by wolves. The children were then sought and found by all the tribe together.

Oyana

The Oyana Indians live in French Guiana and the upper valley of the Paru river in Brazil. They make superb objects out of feathers, head-dresses and breastplates, and these may only be used by those who have undergone the initiation ceremony in silence. They have to endure without complaint the endless stings of wasps and ants which are imprisoned within the breastplate and which are applied to every part of the body in turn.

Palenque

Huge Maya city discovered in the 17th century in the highlands near modern Guatemala. Inside the Temple of the Inscriptions, the great pyramid which towers over the ruins, Alberto Ruz found in 1952 a burial chamber which contained many precious objects in jade and two effigies covered in mosaic. The corridors of the Great Palace which is built around the Observatory show very little of their original ornamentation of coloured stucco. The entire city belongs to the classic period of Maya art.

Posada, José Guadalupe (1852-1913)

Mexican lithographer and zincographer. Posada's genius lies in the fact that he was able to restore to modern Mexico the wonder of her ancient treasures. During a life devoted to the production of over 20,000 pictures, published either in the popular press or on loose sheets, he fought in the most effective way possible against the spiritual block which had hindered Mexican art for over 300 years. No one can really appreciate how much the Mexican revolution owed to Posada. When he was not devoting his talent to actuality, he liked to illustrate the *danse macabre* of popular feast-days in Mexico, an occasion where humour and the utmost seriousness operated in total harmony. This peculiarly Mexican alliance was taken to the heights of modern acuteness in Posada's hands. He was a baker's son and he died poor thanks to his integrity and high standards as an artist.

Potlatch

This outburst of generosity, tinged not a little with sheer ostentation, is a very widespread form of courtesy among the North American Indians. It takes a different tone only in British Columbia, starting in the 19th century, when the practice of giving expensive presents and incurring personal ruin gave way to a more general public destruction which involved the community as a whole in an act of deliberate impoverishment. A sense of competition took over; it was soon necessary to formulate some sort of code in order to preserve the tribes from total bankruptcy. It was decided that only half of the goods accumulated for a potlatch could be destroyed. Apart from its economic aspects (analysed in a masterly fashion by Georges Bataille in *La Part maudite*, *La Consumation*, Paris 1949), the potlatch has an important political aspect: among warrior peoples, it substituted economic competition for physical violence. Among the objects destroyed during the potlatch ceremonies, the most interesting were the engraved and painted copper sheets whose fantastic cost made them particularly suitable for sacrifice. They were ripped up and thrown into the sea.

Pyramids

The fascination of the Egyptian pyramids has added to archæologists' passion for their counterparts in Mexico, Yucatán and Peru. The largest pyramid in the New World is that of Cholula, some 140 feet high, and this is much smaller than the pyramid of Cheops. The imposing nature of the monuments is not related just to size alone. The Mexican pyramid is a ceremonial centre, a place for cult and ritual and has the advantage over its Egyptian counterpart that it is a temple standing high on a series of superimposed platforms. It is not usual to find burial chambers inside their mass. The Maya pyramids are more rectangular and have steeper sides. The temple which stands at their summit usually comprises an acroterium of considerable height. The surface decoration, usually in painted stucco, has disappeared from the great pyramids of central Mexico. In Peru, the largest pyramid of all is that of Moche, which is known as the Pyramid of the Sun. Its neighbour is known as the Pyramid of the Moon and has a series of small inner rooms painted with frescoes.

Quetzalcoatl

The most famous Mexican deity owes his ambiguous character to the practices started by Topiltzin, king of Tula. Proclaiming himself Quetzalcoatl, he introduced the events of his own life into the mythological legends, unconsciously illustrating the theories of Evhemeros, who claimed that gods were really human beings sanctified by the fear and admiration of their subjects. In Nahuatl, Quetzalcoatl means Feathered Serpent, or Bird-Serpent, the bird being the green-feathered quetzal and the snake being the rattlesnake. There are innumerable illustrations of the Feathered Serpent, especially in

Aztec art. They show a serpent coiled around himself, covered in thick plumage. The oldest pictures give Quetzalcoatl jaguar fangs and the jewelled ornaments worn by Mexican dignitaries. Mexican mythology associates the Feathered Serpent with agricultural fertility: maize, rain, the sky, the wind.

Quimbaya

The largest gold objects found in America come from the Quimbaya Indians, who lived in the Colombian highlands between the Magdalena and Cauca rivers. They used beating techniques and *repoussé* work and in addition brought the lost-wax process to perfection by using moulds with internal struts. They used *tumbaga*, an alloy of gold and copper, more than pure gold. Their great technical skill allowed the Quimbaya to cast quite large objects in a rather heavy, soft style, conventional rather than inventive. They were more enterprising in the style of their pottery. To a completely schematic representation of a human being with a face reduced to a simple square, they added a meditative grace and simplicity of posture only achieved by total self-discipline.

Rattles

Objects carved by the Indians of British Columbia. They were the necessary adjuncts of the shamans but were also used for ceremonial purposes by some tribal chiefs. Occasionally they are made from copper, but more usually from cedar wood, the two pieces which form the body being bound together with stitches of cedar-fibre. They come in two main types: some are spheres with handles which reveal two engraved and painted faces when they are raised and lowered; others are in the shape of a bird, on the belly of which a face is carved in bas-relief. On the

bird's back lies the figure of a shaman, and this symbolises his dreams of flight and the relations he has with the spirits, who also appear on the rattle in the shape of birds, the dispensers of all wisdom.

Recuay

The site of Recuay between the Black and White Cordilleras in the Callejón de Huaylas in the north of Peru produced a very special type of pottery, though its relief modelling is not unlike that of Moché. What gives it its unusual characteristic is the painted decoration, which shows stylised animals or geometrical motifs in reserve on a dark background. This painting is usually obtained by a resist technique in black and red on a cream background. Many of the vases show a mixture of mythological allegories and scenes from everyday life with several characters, or else religious ceremonies. On such vases, the figures are modelled in relief and the painting applied with great freedom.

Salish

The southernmost Indian tribe on the North-West Coast of British Columbia, outstanding for the strictness and severity of its art forms. Other tribes whose output has been greater have sought in vain to copy them. Salish art is essentially an art in the service of the shaman, and is probably the most acute form ever devised. The so-called representations of the shaman himself are exteriorisations of his power. This can never be dissolved: it must therefore reappear in a funeral effigy, which acts as its home until such time as a successor to the shaman had been found. The Salish, who lived on the coast of the Georgia Straits and the Juan de Fuca Straits near Victoria and Vancouver, carved tiny and minutely detailed instruments as part of the shaman's equipment.

Sand painting

Among the Hopi Indians, the most authentic heirs of the old Pueblo culture, initiation still takes place in the kivas, where pictures made on the sand with powders show the architecture of the world and the katchinas who rule it. Initiation is preceded by offerings of maize flour. The Navajo took over this practice and gave it tremendous flexibility as they developed it. They have over a hundred traditional patterns for sand paintings, each relating to a special ceremony. The paintings are made at dawn, all the artists together, each casting the colour pigments on the sand with the right hand in a continuous gesture, starting at the centre of the picture and finishing at the outer edge. No painting is kept after sun down. In California, similar paintings have been made on the sand, but with less technical skill. The influence of the Pueblo culture is evident here, for when the Californian Indians prepared for the ceremonies for which the sand paintings were destined, they wore Hopi-style masks.

Santa

According to Rafael Larco Hoyle, the pottery from the Santa valley in the north of Peru probably had its origins in ceramics from the coast and would have been influenced by work from Virú. The people living on the coast probably fled to the mountains before the Mochica invasion, at the period called *Mochica III*, round about A.D. 500. Most of the pottery has positive decoration. Occasionally the motifs include a stylised cat-figure painted in reserve, as found at nearby Recuay. Relief-moulded pottery shows religious scenes, ceremonies and erotic love-play. The Santa culture is without any doubt an intermediary culture between *Virú* and *Mochica III*.

Santarem

The town of Santarem at the confluence of the River Tapajos and the Amazon is the centre of a lost culture which is attributed to the Tapajo Indians. They disappeared before the Portuguese could convert them, and left behind a great number of vases and vessels covered with an intricate mass of animals. Vases with caryatids and vases on pedestals show the same legions of zoomorphic creatures. The Santarem culture pre-dates any efforts by the Portuguese missionaries to influence its style.

Shamanism

The geographical distribution and basic features of shamanism have been discussed by Mircea Eliade in his *Shamanism* (London, 1964). It is a very special view of the world and of the relationships which men have with it. It is also the particular role of the shaman, who established these relationships by means of supranormal or abnormal means. Viewed as a genuine cosmology, shamanism is a basic relief of vast populations (Siberia, Tibet, South-East Asia, Oceania, America, the Artic) and it envisages the possibility of going beyond the limits of usual life as far as time and space are concerned. Journeys to the other world and levitation are the favourite techniques of the shaman, an exceptional being who experiments at a personal level with the most daring possibilities that public consent can grant to the most daring of men.

Tattooing

Body painting achieved by means of permanent dyes seems to be widespread even today in Amazonia and the southern regions of Brazil. Many Indians prefer tattooing to body painting. Some tribes in the Gran Chaco still practise this. During the Pre-Columbian period, it appears that tattooing was common among many nations in Mexico and Peru, though it is difficult to be certain about this when illustrated documents may easily show scarification as well as tattooing. However, those who travelled widely among the North American Indians noted that tattooing by colour pigments was highly esteemed. Eskimos, Haida, Iroquois, Hurons, Osage, Yumans from the Colorado Valley and the Indians from Florida and Virginia were all tattooed, either in small areas or else all over the body. It is interesting that this form of graphic art is no different in style from other plastic arts. Because it is indelible, tattooing is more suitable than body painting for illustrating an individual's life and for showing the relationships he has with the world in general. It was noted that the Indians often associated the tattooing operation with the acquiring of a particular social rank or the successful completion of some exploit or some casual ritual practice which came their way. Because of this, tattooing could indicate either personal dignity or social status.

Teotihuacán

The city of Teotihuacán, some 35 miles from Mexico City, was the greatest ceremonial centre in Mexico, not even excepting Cuicuilco, during the pre-classic period. The culture of Teotihuacán spread its influence as far as Guatemala. Excavations carried out in the city or around it were particularly fruitful in the period 1930-1945. They showed that there were four distinct successive periods in ceramics, covering the time span 200 B.C.-A.D. 900. It was in fact around A.D. 1000 that the civilisation of Teotihuacán disappeared. It was during the 3rd and 7th centuries (in period 3, which corresponds to the height of the Monte Alban culture) that painting and ceramics were at their most brilliant. From this time too come the frescoes of Tepanitla, Tetitla and Atelco; these were very near the great pyramids and Teotihuacán and may well have been the homes of priests and dignitaries. Their ceramics take a distinctive form: they are mostly cylindrical tripod vases. They are usually decorated in imitation *champlevé*. Others, more unusual and more beautiful, were decorated after firing, a technique known as "fresco" decoration. They show the silhouettes of priests and gods and sometimes the face of Tlaloc, the god of rain. This form of vase and decorative technique was known throughout Maya territory. From this moment of Teotihuacán culture comes the fine orange pottery which was carried to greater perfection at a later date.

Tepantitla

A site a few hundred yards from the Pyramid of the Sun at Teotihuacán. It was in 1942 that archæologists uncovered fresco-painted walls showing the paradise of the god of rain, Tlaloc. A crowd of excited people dance over this Tlalocan, a Garden of Eden peopled with butterflies and covered with flowers, maize and cocoa-trees. More recent excavations have revealed more frescoes, and these show two teams of ball-players, each player carrying a stick. The frescoes are thought to date from the classic period of the Teotihuacán culture.

Tepeu

It was during the Tepeu period (A.D. 600-950) that the decoration of Maya ceramics acquired the strength and freedom of line which was to be their essential characteristic. This period is also the one during which the sculpture and architecture of the Old Empire reached its height. Tepeu vases are usually cylindrical. They are painted in red, yellow, black and white on an orange background, the decoration being applied in slip before firing. They show scenes from history or mythology; they are doubtless explained in the accompanying cartouches or bands of hieroglyphics which divide up the painted surface, but these have so far defied all attempts at translation.

Tiahuanaco

The site of Tiahuanaco near Lake Titicaca in Bolivia is now a landscape of ruins dominated by the famous Gateway of the Sun. It was abandoned long before the Incas rose to power and since the 17th century has been systematically despoiled and knocked to the ground. The sphere of influence of what was the most important centre of civilisation in the southern Andes can easily be detected on the map of sites where archæologists have found motifs similar to the Gateway of the Sun or representations of megaliths on pottery, notably in the Nazca region in period B. The fourth phase of Andean culture is therefore known as the Tiahuanaco phase. There has been little excavation at Tiahuanaco itself, but enough pottery has been found for a three-phase classification to be established, the second of these counting as the classic phase. It has a great many zoomorphic vessels representing pumas and llamas with black and white painting on a red base. Goblets, slightly bell-mouthed, are painted inside and show animals, condors, snakes or pumas. The sites of Pucara and Huari may have allowed this style to spread westwards to the coast. When Tiahuanaco reached the stage of art where invention is replaced by imitation, the Tiahuanaco style began to spread even further. Pachacamac was one of the sites influenced most considerably; this was an important centre originally founded in classic times which produced textiles outstanding for the geometricality of their design. Towards the year A.D 1000 Tiahuanaco motifs took over the designs of textiles as well as of ceramic painting all over the coast of Peru.

Tikal

Abandoned in the 9th century like most other Maya cities from the classic period, the great city of Tikal was the greatest of all in the three provinces of the Old Empire. It stands in the present department of Peten in Guatemala. If the date given on the plaque of jade found at Tikal is true (a date corresponding to A.D. 320), Tikal is the oldest Maya city. Many pyramids of considerable height are still standing. Their outlines are abrupt and sharp. They are topped by a temple with thick walls, a place where priests celebrated their rites with such a burning of perfumed gums that holes were left in the walls to let the smoke out. The anthropomorphic perfume burners made in two sections are typical of the classical ceramics of Peten. The lintels of the inside doors of the temples are made from carved wood at Tikal, as they are at Uaxactun, a satellite town founded by people from Tikal. They were responsible for an original concept of associating steles and stone altars. At Tikal, many steles have been discovered. They are engraved or covered with stucco which was once polychrome. Tikal pottery, like all pottery from the central territory of the Maya, was influenced by Teotihuacán both in form and painting technique.

Tizatlan

This Mexican site was the capital of a small state of Nahuatl-speaking people which managed to avoid Aztec suzerainty in spite of its proximity to Tenochtitlán. Tizatlan may have been a colony from Cholula, a great cultural centre and the sacred city of the Mixtec people. Frescoes on the lateral walls of two sacrificial altars have been found at Tizatlan. They depict the God of Death. The colours and the way the figures are drawn are very similar to the art of the Codex Borgia.

Tlaloc

God of all kinds of moisture among the Mexicans. The dryness of the highlands and the use of cultivated plants for feeding city-dwellers are apparently responsible for the veneration of this legendary rain-maker. His attributes, especially his odd spectacle-rimmed eyes, were common in Mexican art from the pre-classic period onwards and lasted till the conquest. At Teotihuacán, the building known as the Temple of Quetzalcoatl, which is really just the lower platform of a pyramid whose upper floors have disappeared, shows the head of Tlaloc alternating with serpent-heads all over the western façade. The frescoes devoted to Tlaloc at Teotihuacán also show various stylised attributes. At Tepantitla is a painting of Tlalocan, the Rain God's Paradise, full of flowers and gaiety. Mexican symbolism associated the colour green and jade stones with Tlaloc. Among the Maya, the Goddess of the Waters, who was known as the Lady with the Green Stone Skirt, was thought to be Tlaloc's sister.

Tula

In the history of old Mexico, the period which saw the abandonment of the city of Teotihuacán was followed shortly afterwards by an event of no less importance. This was the arrival of the Toltecs, who came from the north to invade the region around the present Mexico City, settling first at Culhuacan, then at Tula, 50 miles to the north of Mexico City in the year A.D. 980. Legend says that the king-priest of Tula who had taken the name Quetzalcoatl abandoned Tula in 999, went to Yucatán and then founded Chichén Itzá, building it on the same ground plan as Tula. The population of Tula fled towards the south in 1168 and the city has been abandoned ever afterwards. Excavations began in 1931, and have not so far been able to suggest why the city became so outstandingly important as a religious and artistic centre in such a very short space of time. Tula ceramics are usually found in the shape of bowls decorated with the attributes of Quetzalcoatl. The most marvellous piece of pottery so far discovered at Tula is a representation of a fish or perhaps a snake holding a human head in its jaws; this terracotta is covered with mother-of-pearl mosaic, each piece as big as a fingernail. At Tula, the pyramids were of modest size. Graphic art was limited to the carving of the famous cylindrical or square pillars: these still stand and give a vivid impression of what the great colonnade must have looked like. Apart from purely decorative motifs, there are the symbols of Quetzalcoatl, jaguar-figures, prairie wolves, eagles tearing a heart to pieces, snakes with bells devouring skeletons. This last motif is remarkably like the popular art of modern Mexico. The oldest representation of Chacmool is to be found at Tula. This god was to be found wherever the Toltecs passed, a youth lying elegantly on his elbow with a plate held at stomach-level;

he appears again at Chichén Itzá, where he is one of the great attractions.

Weaving

When the Spaniards arrived in the New World, they were extremely surprised to find that the people they had imagined went naked did nothing of the sort. Mexican warriors fought protected by surcoats of woven cotton an inch thick, which were well able to resist the obsidian-pointed arrows which shattered the Spanish armour. There was no people in America which did not know how to weave, even if the use of cloth for garments might be fairly rudimentary. Material was in open-weave and close-weave on frames with no lower bar. The width of Peruvian cloth which cannot be obtained on mechanical frames needed the collaboration of many weavers placed side by side, working in relays to pass the shuttle from one side to the other. The textiles used are very varied. The Indians from British Columbia used a warp of cedar fibres and a weft of goat's wool. The Salish bred a special kind of dog for its hair and sheared them like sheep. The Mexicans wove fibres from sisal, palm-trees, rabbit-fur and hare-fur for the finest of their textiles. Cotton was in greatest use. Only the Huaxtecs were able to supply it. For the Mexicans, the Mother of the Gods was also the Mistress of Cotton. In Peru, sisal and cotton were woven as they were in Mexico, but they also used llama wool, alpaca and vicuña. The Inca's ceremonial tunics were woven from vicuña and bat-hairs. The animal origin of Peruvian textiles has contributed considerably to their state of preservation. Mexican textiles have not been so lucky, on account of the relative humidity of the climate. We do know, however, that Mexican weavers produced cloth of superb texture and that their skill in dyeing was even greater than that of the Peruvians, whose burial blankets, especially those found at Paracas, reveal their artistry in the wide variety of colours as well as the richness of decoration. One single burial blanket had no fewer than one hundred and ninety different colours, and to produce them, the Peruvians had to use every single technique known to man. Not only did they weave the finest cloth ever made, apart from Coptic textiles, but they also made gauze, satin-stitch embroidery with wool threaded on cotton and a sort of thick jersey-material which involved the use of knotted threads. The famous mummy No. 49 from Paracas Necropolis was found to wear eleven cloaks, twenty ponchos or shirts, eleven skirts, six head-cloths, and twenty pieces of self-coloured cloth. The largest of all was 30 yards long and 4 yards wide. All the motifs of the decorated textiles agree in colour as well as in symbolic value.

Yucatán

The territory formerly occupied by the Mayas comprises three distinct geographical zones. The southern one is a zone of high fertile mountains, separated from the Pacific by a coastal plain; it shows little trace of Maya culture. The finest and most beautiful Maya cities from the classic period of the Empire are found in the central zone, in the Petén department, the state of Chiapas and on the frontier of British Honduras. The northern zone, which is formed by the chalky peninsula of Yucatán, shows fewer traces of this period than of the so-called Maya Renaissance. This period started with the Toltec invasion and from it date not only the city of Chichén Itzá but also the palace of the Governor at Uxmal, whose façade is decorated with a mosaic frieze, and the façades of Hochob, covered with serpent-masks surrounding doorways in the walls.